Gentle Thoughts
for
Daily Living

Written by
Lois M. Sunley

PublishAmerica
Baltimore

First printing

To Isabel

Love and Light

Lois

Aug 2005

ISBN: 1-4137-6100-3
PUBLISHED BY PUBLISHAMERICA, LLLP
www.publishamerica.com
Baltimore

Printed in the United States of America

With loving thanks to my loved ones on this side and the other, for the insights printed on these pages.

A loving thank you to Phil Michael, for all his help in putting these pages into perfect order.

The day has just begun
Count the hours one by one.
Watch the minutes race away.
Is life over?
Is it done?
No! Never!
The day has just begun!

Time marches on
With or without us.

Take time each day
To see all the beauty
In your life.

Lazy days are our gift to our soul.
Relax…enjoy…smile!

7

Smile on me
And I'll smile on you.

Moon light…starlight
Candle light…and firelight
All reflect in your eyes
Sharing their brilliance and beauty
Magnifying yours.

People's hearts are warmed by the touch
You can almost taste the beauty in a still night
With the quiet of the twinkling stars and
The murmur of the breeze
Through the trees.

Happiness is always just a touch away…
We touch each other's lives in many ways…
We can touch a heart with a smile or a warm gesture.
The beauty in nature touches our soul…
The love we feel fills us up and makes us strong.

When you feel desolate
Quiet yourself and know
Deep within that you are
Not alone.
Feel the universal love.

People gravitate to the light:
The light of
…love
…laughter
…our higher power.

We are all given special moments of happiness.
It's up to us to recognize them
And enjoy them as they are given.

Life can be heaven on earth
Or hell on earth.
The choice is up to us.

Beauty is precious.
Beauty of the mind.
Beauty of the soul.
Beauty of the heart.
Cherish your beauty and
The beauty of others.

Revere beauty and let it fill you with joy!

Music makes my heart sing
And my soul dance.

Wonderful things happen in life
To people who do more than exist
They participate.

Creativity surges when you free your mind
Of all the cluttering negative meanderings
Of your thoughts

Happiness is sprinkled liberally on positive people.
Negativity creates a rain of disappointments.

Life is full of wonder.
There is beauty in wonder.
There is creativity in wonder.
To wonder is to live.

A smile from the heart
Touches the soul.

A special place is where you can go
To learn more about yourself.
To learn more about yourself helps
You accept yourself
And learn to love yourself.
Find your special place.

Sometimes sadness can cover you in a thick fog
But eventually the sun will break through and chase
All the coldness away and leave
You warmed and alive again.

When you are sad and it rains
You feel as if the world is crying with you.
When you are happy and the sun shines
You feel as if the world is rejoicing with you.

Accept everyone unconditionally.
When you are accepted unconditionally
You feel better in your own skin…
Help others feel that way too.

Pain creates growth.
When you learn from pain
The growth makes you stronger.

Lean on others
When you need to
But
Remember you are the
Strongest person you know.

Laughter is lightness,
Crying with pain is darkness.

You awake from the darkness of pain
To the joyousness of health.

Memories can fill us with a happy peace
Or drown us in discontent.
Some are motivators,
Some we allow to stunt our growth.
Which would you rather have?

Sleep is nourishment
For our minds and bodies.
To dream is to create.
To experience pain is to grow.
To learn is to live.
To forgive is to accept.
To forget opens you to love.
To be happy, we need to love
And accept ourselves.

To breathe is to have life,
To dream is to create.
To experience pain is to grow.
To learn is to live.
To forgive is to accept.
To forget opens you to love.
To be happy, we need to love
And accept ourselves.

Days are brighter, laughter deeper
Smiles reach your eyes
Relationships are sweeter
When you believe in you
And see the beauty in yourself
As God made you…
Totally unique and wondrous.

When we open our minds
We see the many blessings
In our lives.
When we open our hearts
It fills and overflows with love.

Let the sunshine in your heart
Send out rays of love to
All you meet.
Everyone needs to feel the
Warmth of unconditional love.

When you are in love the world is full of colors,
They shine brilliantly through your eyes and
Bounce off everything in your sight.
Love yourself and watch your world shine.

Loved ones are the decorations
On our tree of life…
We enjoy them all year long
But appreciate them more
As our trees grow.

My soul basks in the
Warmth of yours.

Sometimes when our hearts ache
We think we are unlovable.
Love for us starts within us
Not from outside us, from others.
Always love you and others will too.

When we trust we can fully love.

Light shines from our eyes.
Memories linger in our minds.
Our hearts dance
And
Our souls sing out loud
When we are in love,
Whether it's the love of another
Or
Love of the world.
We rejoice inside and out.

Love is like a raindrop
Joining with another
Growing ever stronger
Nurturing the soul.

When your focus in a relationship
Is for the other to be happy…
And they feel the same way…
That is love!

Sweet air caressing smoldering
Ashes excites the fire
To blaze once more.
Just like sweet words whispered
Softly can bring dying love
Back to burning desire.

Old loves don't die…
They live on…
For eternity
Within our soul.
When we return…
We recognize the old love.
We may not know why.
But our soul knows.

The early stage of love is like a raindrop
Fragile and shining with beauty.
When it falls it can either
Shatter into a million fragmented drops
Or
Develop into a lovely shimmering lake.
In this lake, all can share the love and beauty,
Animals and humans alike.
Just as your love can continue to grow
And reach out and nourish all you touch.

The thought of love
Can put stars in your eyes.
The gift of love
Puts sunshine in your heart.

Tears fill my heart when love leaves.
Joy fills my heart when love returns.

The song in my heart
Sings my love for you
In the same lilting notes
Of the birds in spring.

Sweet nothings whispered in the dark
Give you more warmth
Than the thickest blanket.

Your soul warms mine when our hearts entwine.

The comforting energy in your arms
As you hold me
Brings me total peace
And contentment.
Incredible kisses…indelible memories!

Loss of an old love can bring so much pain
But when the special happy memories of a
Time past come back, the joy of love gives
Your heart the hug it needs.

When people leave your life,
To ease the pain,
Look inside your heart
And see the many blessings
This joining has given you.

I know you,
Maybe not your name,
Maybe not your face,
But I recognize your soul.
We are old friends.
Maybe that is why
I don't remember names.
In reality…
They aren't important.
They are just a means
To identify us to others
Like an I.D. number,
But not a necessity for
Our souls for recognition.

My life is an open book.
Is yours?
Share your knowledge,
Learn from others,
Expand your experiences.
Through others you can grow.
You don't have to
Experience pain first hand
To learn.
Don't hold in your joy
Or
Your pain.
Open your life to others.
Be available for them
To be open to you too.

In the breath of time
We measure our lives
In moments …
Fleeting whispers of happiness
And blinks of sadness
Life speeds along
And we enjoy
The ride.

Time spent raising our children is like a breath
In the space of our time on earth.

Children are the flowers of our lives.
Teach them to be responsible,
Shower them with much love,
And watch them grow.

When you build "walls"
You hide your gentle soul.
We are all born with
A gentle soul.
Try to let your gentleness
Spread out and touch
The world around you.

Each person we meet and greet
Helps us in some small way.
Sometimes they help us
Have tremendous growth
And sometimes it's almost
Intangible.
But even a smile
From a stranger on the street
Affects how we see ourselves on
Any given day.
Share your smiles,
Share your love,
See how it reflects
Back at you.

Stepping stones are what help us
Maneuver through the pitfalls of life.
These stones may be made up of
Family and friends
Our education
Our learning
Our faith.
But wherever they come from
They are here to help us move
From one experience,
One growth pattern
To another.
Bless the path you are on.
Love the person you are becoming.
Remember with love the person you were.
And relax into your life.
Know that you are where you are meant to be.

Thank you for opening your heart
And
Embracing my soul in friendship.

Lovers can come and go
Friendships can last a lifetime.
Never take a friend for granted
Or it may be the end of that
Gift of friendship.

The warmth of the sun
Can never warm you as much
As the warmth of true love
And unconditional friendship.

Friends are like the gems on the jewelry
Of our lives' experiences.
Some are diamonds
And
Some are pearls.

True friends never leave your heart
Even if the distance separates you
And life gets in the way…
Preventing regular contact.
Friendship is constant
No matter how much
Your life changes.

Renewal of old friendships warms our heart.
Look up an old friend and give them joy.

Love can ebb and flow
In and out of your life.
Friendships that are true
Last a lifetime through.

External beauty comes from
The light within us.

As the bloom of youth
Fades into the past
Our inner beauty
Shines through
At last.

Youth feeds age…
Age nurtures youth.
Combining youth and age
Creates wisdom.

Open your senses.
Smell, taste, touch, and see
The beauty in your life.

To get angry is part of life
To forgive and forget is a gift to yourself.

Try to dance through your life,
The steps will get easier...
Hear the music in your heart.

We are never inadequate in the eyes of God.
We are loved for ourselves
With all our imperfections.

Whoever said life was a bowl of cherries
Forgot about the stomachaches.

Kindness to others
Is the salve
That helps others heal.

Life is a continuance of learning.
To not learn is to not live.

Real people are humans with issues.
They acknowledge and learn from these issues,
As best they can.

Being open and honest is a conscious choice.

Knowledge learned or experienced is a gift.
When we take off our blinders of fear
The growth knowledge is phenomenal.

When we share our lives and experiences
We show we care beyond just ourselves.

Age is a number and a lesson we have to accept.
We all grow older and can only hope
We grow wiser too.

The world doesn't revolve around us.
We are just the spokes in the wheel.
We try to keep our course in life
As trim as we can.
At times we wobble
And then...
There are the glorious times
We turn true.

Life is full of surprises,
The smile of a stranger,
The kiss of a lover,
The hug of a child.
All so beautiful…
Making you feel so "right."

A gift from the heart
Make the stars shine
In our eyes.

It's hard to find life's opportunities
If you keep your feet on the ottoman.

Let your worries fall away
Like the dying petals on a flower.

Filter out the negative.
Let the positive consume you
Every waking moment of your day.

Expectations can create thoughts of happiness.
Reality can leave us empty.
We need to make our expectations
Our reality.

To be able to trust
Is a beautiful thing.
Be conscious in your trust.
To be unconscious
Can blind you to the facts
That might hurt you.

Life is like a flower in bloom.
Each time we share ourselves,
Each time we allow ourselves to love,
We open the petals more
And share our glorious inner beauty.

May all your hopes and dreams
Become your realities.

May your tree of life be filled
With blessings and love.

May the angels touch your heart
With happiness and peace.

As you near your final journey
On this place we call earth
Your eyes become clearer and more iridescent
Reflecting the beauty of your soul
Enabling others to catch a glimpse
Of what lies beyond
Waiting for all of us.
Total sacred peace.

Printed in the United States
30674LVS00005B/394-492

9 781413 761009